F.R.O.G.I.E.

Fully Rely on God in Everything

A COLLECTION
OF POETRY TO ENLIGHTEN, INSPIRE,
AND ENCOURAGE

by Aimee Boisot

PublishAmerica
Baltimore

© 2008 by Aimee Boisot.
All rights reserved. No part of this book may be reproduced, stored in a retrieval system or transmitted in any form or by any means without the prior written permission of the publishers, except by a reviewer who may quote brief passages in a review to be printed in a newspaper, magazine or journal.

First printing

PublishAmerica has allowed this work to remain exactly as the author intended, verbatim, without editorial input.

ISBN: 1-60474-957-1
PUBLISHED BY PUBLISHAMERICA, LLLP
www.publishamerica.com
Baltimore

Printed in the United States of America

Dear Reader,

There are so many people who have inspired the poems in this book. I would like to thank my church family at Olive Branch Baptist Church in Blackridge VA. With special thanks to the praise team I sing with Trish, Joanne, Carl and Brian. I love you all! Thank you for your support. And thanks also to my Sunday school class, the cards and prayers during the rough times lifted my spirits tremendously. Pastor Micheal and Pastor Anthony your phone calls and concern are always comforting.

To my friend Rene who had to endure my constant reading of my poetry. You've always found a way to keep me laughing when I least felt like it.

To my family with which God has so richly blessed me my sisters Dana, Kelly and Sheri and my mom and Dad. Without their constant support I would not be where I am today. To my son Spencer who inspired many of theses poems, I love you, and count it a privilege to be your mom. Last and most important I thank the Lord. He has seen me through many battles and will see me through many more I'm sure.

I hope these poems will offer some hope and encouragement to all who read them. May the Lord use my words to comfort those who are hurting, and find those who are lost.
God Bless!
Aimee Boisot

ON REPENTANCE & FORGIVENESS

All the prophets testify about him that everyone who believes in him receives forgiveness of sins through his name.
Acts 10:43

I have not come to call the righteous, but sinners to repentance.
Luke 5:32

Forgiveness

*Dark skies surround the quiet of night
An eerie calm settles on the lone figure
standing in the shadows
Without warning the skies split
and rain pours down
in torrents
drenching the invader
The silence is broken
by the thundering of the falling rain
as puddles form at the feet
and cool mud splashes
the naked soul
As suddenly as it started
it's over
Moonlight traces a tear
down a solemn face
and all is quiet
Forgiveness has been given
The figure
no longer a stranger
Embraces the light and walks
in the Glory of God*

Christ's Love Never Fails

Sometimes people change
We may even lose a friend
But Christ's love is something
On which we can depend
He keeps no record of wrongs
He's there to listen to you
when He says your sin's forgiven
He means forgotten too
People sometimes fail us
as we ourselves may do
But God will never fail
He'll always be there for you

Seven Little Letters

*Seven little letters
In two little words
They aren't so hard to say
So why have so many people failed
To say them just today
They could make the difference
To one who has been wronged
But often they go unsaid
for entirely too long
We shrug our shoulders and walk away
And we say this instead
They know I didn't mean it
I'll talk to them real soon
We've all used these excuses
And heard this little tune
Everybody makes mistakes
Of this we can be sure
But if we fail to say I'm sorry
The friendship is no more
Seven little letters
In two little words
They aren't so hard to say
So if you need to say them
Make sure you do
TODAY*

At the Cross

Peace is found
At the cross
Mercy is found
At the cross
Guidance is found
At the cross
Acceptance is found
At the cross
Love is found
At the cross
Grace is found
At the cross
Comfort is found
At the cross
Patience is found
At the cross
Forgiveness is found
At the cross
Come to the cross

I Stand at Your Door and Knock

I come to You empty
broken and poor
I have nothing to offer
as I knock on your door
But You oh Lord
the most gracious host
Usher me in
with all of my ghost
The ghost of my sins
that follow me here
cower in your presence
and shake with fear
I ask for forgiveness
and you cast them aside
the sins all scatter
and try to hide
You destroy them all
for you have seen
witch way they went
and you make me clean
Back through your door
I walk much lighter
My relationship with you
has grown much tighter
Your grace I will always
carry with me
And spread Your Word
that others may see
That they too may have
forgiveness of sin
If they open their heart
and just let You in

ON
HIS WORLD
&
HIS CREATIONS

With my great power and outstretched arm I made the earth and it's people and the animals that are on it, and I give it to anyone I please
Jeremiah 27:5

A Cool Autumn Morning

*Autumn leaves fall crisp
to the ground
The wind gently rustling
the only sound
Bright morning sunlight
filtering through
canopies of red
and orange on blue
The smell of my coffee
permeates the air
At the beauty of the morning
I breath deep and stare
Each day more brisk
than the one before
Giving a hint as to
what lies in store
Soon to be nothing
but gray, black and white
For now I'll just bask in
the glorious sight*

Two Shadows Dancing

Soft shadows on the ground below
mingle with the clean white snow
The images darken than quickly fade
as clouds roll in to offer shade
A gentle wind across the sky
gives the shadows another try
Quickly they come out to play
before the clouds can come and stay
They turn and twist and shake and roll
happy for the time they stole
To stretch and fade then darker grow
will too soon end they both do know
A soft sweet giggle is heard on the breeze
as the shadows dance off into the trees

Snow Storm

*Magical crystals
that dance on the air
They glisten and glitter
and stick in your hair
Catching the sunlight
sending out rays
of cascading rainbows
on backgrounds of grays
Pinging so softly
on roof tops of tin
sing you to sleep
as the storm begins*

Autumn Memories

*Falling, twisting
Tumbling down
Bright fall colors
of red, orange and brown
Cracking and crunching
under your shoe
Scraping the sidewalk
and landing on you
Raking and piling
as high as you dare
Jumping and laughing
without any care
Tossing the leaves
that land with a sigh
Breathing in air that
is cool and is dry
Enjoying the beauty
as earth prepares to sleep
Theses are the memories
that we will always keep*

Summer Nights

The moon that is shinning
reflects on the pond
Sending sparkling ripples
Far and beyond
The duck that sleeps
In the rushes by night
The evening is a peaceful sight
Crickets are chirping
Croaking frogs can be heard
The great white owl whoing
the only bird
The rest are all asleep
in their nest
Theses warm summer nights
are truly blessed

Summertime

Blue, purple, yellow
Dance in the sun
Flowers that tickle
Your legs as you run
Sweet smelling grass
That's freshly been mowed
Catches a breeze
And drifts to your nose
Bare feet that softly tread
Over the path
That's wound like a thread
Days that are longer
Nights that are warm
Silence that's broken
By quick thunderstorms
Times for friendship,
Laughter and fun
Quick let us go
Before summer is done

From Day into Night

The sun shining brightly
Warming my skin
Bright rays that fill
the emptiness within
Short shadows that stretch
as the day starts to fade
Twisting and turning as
through them I wade
Cool breezes that blow
as night begins to fall
The crickets awake
you can hear their call
The sun goes to sleep
and the moon shines bright
I whisper a prayer
and say goodnight

Cody

*Fuzzy and furry
snuggling close
Purring and pawing
then bites at my toes
Quick as lightening
he jumps on the dog
then onto the window sill
just like a frog
He tears through the house
with a blur of white
It really is a comical sight
Then all at once
he curls up in your lap
And settles down
for a little cat nap*

ON COMING TO CHRIST & THE SECOND COMING

But these are written that you may believe that Jesus is the Christ, the Son of God and that by believing you may have life in his name.
John 20:31

At that time the sign of the Son of Man will appear in the sky, and all the nations of the earth will mourn. They will see the Son of Man coming on the clouds of the sky, with power and great glory.
Matthew 24:30

Someday My Prince Will Come

Someday my Prince will come
We've all heard this before
But the Prince that I am waiting for
Won't be coming through the door
From the heavens He'll be coming
On some fine glorious day
We do not know the year or hour
But the bible tells the way
He'll ride on a cloud glory
The trumpets all will sound
And all the Christians will disappear
Not one will be around
So if you want to join us
In heaven for eternity
These are the steps to follow
So you will be with me
Pray these words in earnest
Mean everything you say
And you'll become a child of God
And be saved right away
Lord I know I am a sinner
I'm sorry I've done wrong
Please forgive me Lord I pray
I've waited far too long
I believe that Jesus Christ your son
Was crucified and died
He rose three days latter
And now he is alive
He died to save me from my sins
His blood washed them away
And now I ask you Lord to please
Come into my heart to stay

He's Coming Back for Me

A Christians life's not easy
It isn't always fun
We live in a world of evil
Many don't know God's Son
Sin is all around us
It's accepted as the norm
But if we hold tight to Jesus
He'll carry us through the storm
Don't forget His promise
That there will come a day
When all the pain has ended
And all sorrows gone away
He'll come back to get us
The dead in Christ He'll raise
And all Christians that are living
Will be gathered up in praise
He'll take us all to heaven
Our Lord's sweet face we'll see
And we will live in joy and peace
For all eternity

Baptism

Dying unto self
I arise with thee
Reborn renewed
a new creature to be
No longer in darkness
left to roam
In me Jesus has
made his home
Signed sealed and delivered
by God above
soaring to new heights
like a graceful white dove
I make this public
profession to all
Come join me now
and heed His call
Then when life's last
breath you take
In Jesus' arms
you shall awake

Coming to Christ

That's not normal
so they say
What is normal anyway
She can't remember
the hour or day
that she decided
she felt this way
Spinning and falling
out of control
trying so hard
to gain a hold
Slipping and sliding
without any clue
How in the world
will she get through
Then from a friend
she hears of Christ
She learns from her
of his sacrifice
How he died on the cross
to save us from sin
She too can be saved
if she just lets Him in
She asks for forgiveness
believes in His name
And basks in His glory
She won't be the same
No her troubles don't all
disappear on the spot
But now when she falls
In His arms she'll be caught
She doesn't have
to bear things alone
God's there to help her
He's always at home

Come Dwell in Me

Sometimes I feel so far away
Locked inside myself I stay
Troubles seem to weigh me down
Too much my smiles turn to frowns
Here are my burdens oh Lord of mine
Take them from me and make then thine
Shoulder the weight and bring me from under
These clouds of doubt and rumbling thunder
Please keep the devil far far away
And all my worries keep them at bay
For with you I know I can do all things
You are the one to whom my heart sings
Help me to remember in times of doubt
You can calm my spirit throughout
Help me to put all my trust in you
And sing your sweet praises in all that I do
Unlock my heart and set me free
Come inside and dwell in me

ON RELYING ON CHRIST

When you pass through the waters, I will be with you; and through the rivers, they shall not overwhelm you; when you walk through the fire you shall not be burned, and the flame shall not consume you.
Isaiah 43:2

Do not conform any longer to the pattern of this world, but be transformed by the renewing of your mind. Then you will be able to test what God's will is—his good pleasing and perfect will.
Romans 12:2

In the Stillness

*In the stillness I wait for You
The quiet of the night
broken only by my heart beat
I take all my troubles
and lay them at your feet
And wait for you to meet me here
and fill me with your peace
I listen in the darkness
and I hear you calling to me
calling all who are thirsty
all who are weary and worn
to come drink the living water
rest our heads on your shoulder
and be renewed in You
In the stillness I wait for You
and I know You're here
I feel Your arms around me
And I am restored*

The Author of Life

*The author of life
who wrote my story
hears my prayers
and calms my worries
He knows the deepest
parts of my soul
He holds me close
when life takes it's toll
He smiles softly
as He comforts in fright
He gently guides me
through darkest of night
He knows just how
each chapter will start
Every breath every sigh
every beat of my heart
He knows how everything
will turn out in the end
So I'll learn to trust
My God and my friend*

From Thunder to Gardens

Voices like thunder
Sharp words as lightening
Storms that tear us apart
Hurtful phrases that pour
From clouds of anger
Only meant to destroy and retort
Without God as our stronghold
Our rock and our anchor
This could be us my friend
But allow Him to get
To the heart of the problem
And it will work out in the end
Soft whispering rain
gently falling
Words spoken with love
And with care
With each cleansing shower
A garden is growing
When discussions are peacefully shared

You Have a Plan

*Sometimes bad things happen
and even though we pray
Everything just might not
exactly go our way
But you oh Lord know better
You know exactly what we need
Sometimes prayers aren't answered
'cause they don't fulfill your deed
You hear us when we're hurting
You hold us in your hand
If we place our trust in You
the outcome will be grand
So guide us through each day
Help us heed your call
Though we may not understand
You have a plan for all*

Reflections

Softly she walks
through the forest so still
head hanging low
the birds singing shrill
She stops at the edge
of the pond glistening bright
And the reflection she sees
gives a startling fright
The face looking back
both worn and tattered
Gives insight into
a life that is shattered
She looks as a stranger
appears at her side
her eyes bright and cheery
with nothing to hide
She looks quite familiar
and it's then that she knows
the girl that she's looking at
is her long ago
before the world
got the better of her
when she was a child
happy, confident and sure
but now the world

(continued)

*has taken over her life
and she greets each morning
with worry and strife
She sighs as she realizes
all that she's lost
she'd go back if she could
no matter the cost
Then the young girl
from long ago grins
you don't have to go back
I'm still deep within
Just look inside
and let me shine through
and find the strength
that you used to hold onto
Don't rely on yourself
when life brings you sorrow
and struggle and worry
about tomorrow
But have the faith
as you did long ago
Trust in the Lord
and let His light show*

Through Good Times and Bad

When all is peaceful
When all is calm
We oft forget to praise You
When all is happy
And nothings wrong
We oft forget to thank you
But when tragedy
And sorrow strike
It's to You that we turn
Maybe that's why
Bad things happen
To help us grow and learn
To rely on Christ in all we do
To thank Him everyday
Not just in the stressful times
When things don't go our way

Put Your Trust in Jesus

*When life gets you down
and you think you can't cope
Remember where
to place your hope
When things go wrong
and you can't find your way
and you don't know why
things happened today
Remember to put
your trust in the Lord
And He'll supply you
with great reward
Rely on Jesus
When you don't understand
Look to Him for guidance
Reach out and take His hand
Though He may not show you
What to expect
His way is perfect
and you He protects
So when you get discouraged
and the going gets too tough
Rely on the Lord
To get you through this stuff*

Sometimes I Cry

Sometimes life
can be too much
Wandering aimlessly
out of touch
Reaching and grasping
without any clue
Of just what I'm trying
to hold onto
Sometimes I cry
without physical pain
My emotions are spent
I feel I'm going insane
I cry till the depths
of my soul starts to shake
God hears from His throne
He can feel my heart break
He reaches to calm
His child with His touch
It's awesome to know
He loves me so much
He picks up the pieces
that broke and tore
and puts them back stronger
then ever before
I can go on
now that I know
That God is with me
wherever I go

Lost and Found

Lost in the darkness
Stumbling through
Trying to make it
Without You
Finding my own path
making my way
In the wrong direction
With prices to pay
From one bad turn
into the next
No one to turn to
no sign of rest
Then at the bottom
of my despair
I call on You Lord
and You find me there
You pick me up
set me on the right track
The skies that I see
are no longer black
No longer in darkness
I walk in Your light
With you to guide me
down paths that are right

Lost in the Storm

Often times I wonder
what God intends for me
Sometimes I feel I'm drowning
Lost upon the sea
I have no sense of direction
I don't know which way to go
The waves tower above me
and toss me to and fro
I pray to God for guidance
I look to Him in prayer
but there are times that I feel
that there is no one there
Then through the tidal wave
a life line comes to me
And through the raging storm
He pulls me to safety
For though I may not hear Him
He's always close to me
To love me and to guide me
Through all eternity

No Greater Friend

No other friend like Jesus
has ever been so true
He knows everything about you
And yet He still loves you
He knows your darkest secret
and the things you try to hide
He is a perfect listener
in whom you can confide
He never will betray you
He'll always remain true
And if you let Him lead your life
He'll bring out the best in you
More than you can imagine
More than you can say
His love for you is perfect
In every single way

My King and Shepherd

Your amazing grace surrounds me
Your perfect peace enfolds
You loving mercy comforts
with strength that is so bold
I stand in awe and wonder
at the feet of my Great King
And marvel at the beauty
and the calmness that you bring
Into his flock I'm taken
My heart and life He'll mend
And He will always guide me
Master, Shepherd, friend

You Are Always with Me

When dark skies surround me
And I can't see the light
Help me to remember
You have me in your sight
You're always right beside me
Your never far away
You'll catch me when I'm falling
And with me you will stay
You hold me when I'm crying
And dry my weary tears
You whisper in the darkness
And calm my raging fears
My burdens You will carry
I lay them at your feet
They are no longer mine to bear
They can not claim defeat
Soon the skies begin to clear
The clouds roll out of sight
I take Your hand and walk away
Everything will be alright

ON
LIVING LIKE CHRIST

"Whoever welcomes one of these little children in my name welcomes me; and whoever welcomes me does not welcome me but the one who sent me."
Mark 9:37

Did I Make You Proud

Tomorrow is not a promise
or next week a guarantee
Today is what we're given
our focus it must be
Not to dwell on what has happened
or what we want to see
But did I do enough today
to make You proud of me?
Each day that we are given
every second of the day
presents the opportunity
to show someone the way
Did I try to make it better?
Did I grumble and complain?
Did I offer some encouragement
or cause somebody's pain?
Did I do my best to make the most
of what I have inside?
Or did I turn the other way
and instead try to hide?
Help me to be positive,
loving, kind and good
To use each moment wisely
and do the things I should
To build up and encourage
and be the best that I can be
and do enough everyday
to make You proud of me

He's Always There

*When no one else cares
and no one hears your cry
Your worlds turned upside down
and you can't understand why
When your pillow at night
is the one to dry your tears
and there seems to be no end
to your trials and your fears
When you don't have a friend
in whom you can confide
and your problems tend to pile up
and you want to run and hide
God hears you and He reaches down
and holds you close at heart
He comforts and assures you
from you He won't depart
So when you feel discouraged
and you feel that no one cares
remember that God loves you
He will always be there*

Do They See You in Me?

Yesterday I think I saw you
Standing by a tree
In a child who stopped to help
A friend who scrapped his knee
Last week I thought I caught a glimpse
Of your smile so loving sweet
In a wrinkled face who bought a meal
For a man with nothing to eat
I think it was on Thursday
You were standing in the rain
You'd given your umbrella
To an old man in great pain
Was it Tuesday you gave up your seat
To the pregnant lady on the bus?
It was a long and bumpy ride
but you never made a fuss
Last night I lay in bed and thought
of all the places you'd been
In regular people who took the time
to share the love within
If I see you in all of them
I had to stop and see
Do I do your work throughout my day
Do they see you in me?

Into His Light

*Into His light
with outstretched hands
I walk to where
My Savior stands
Well done my good
and faithful one
Welcome home
your job is done
He welcomes me
into his embrace
At last, at last
I see his face*

Do Unto Others

*When you saw me hungry
Did you offer me some bread
Or did you walk away
and ignore me instead
When you saw me hurting
Did you comfort and lift up
Or did you say your hopeless
Forget it just give up
For if you saw someone in need
and passed without a thought
Then you also walked by me
ignoring what I've taught
Do onto others
as you'd have done to you
Open your heart and
let My light shine through
If you expect me to be there
When you need me
Then be there for others
When they need you to be*

ON
PRAISING GOD
&
HIS GIFTS

I will extol the Lord at all times;
his praise will always be on my lips
Psalms 34:1

For Jesus answered her, "If you knew the gift of God and who it
that asks you for a drink, you would have asked him and he would
have given you living water."
John 4:10

How Long, Oh Lord

How many mornings
have I opened my eyes
And not taken the time
to praise you
How many times
have I seen the sun rise
And not stopped
to thank you
How many meals
have I eaten in haste
and not paused
to pray to you
How much of my life
have I taken for granted
forgetting the one
who made me
How much longer
will I continue this way
before I remember
my creator
Remind me oh Lord
to stop each day
and take the time
to praise you
to pray everyday
and never forget
to give thanks
to my savior

Take Time

You paint a glorious sunset
at the close of each day
For those who take time to notice
You wind paths through trees
and meadows of flowers
For those who take time to follow them
You send birds to sing
a sweet melody
For those who take time to listen
You bring people
who could change lives
For those who get to know them
You send us gifts everyday
so many are taken for granted
So remind me today to
Notice your sunset
Follow your path
Listen to your birds
And cherish the friends I am given

Like Gold Through the Fire

*When life comes at you
headed full force
and your lost and scared
and completely off course
When you can't figure out
witch end is up
and your tired and really
just want to give up
When there's no one there
to dry all your tears
and you wake at night
consumed by your fears
Remember the Lord
who gave you all things
and praise Him in spite
of the hardship life brings
For God will not leave you
alone in the battle
He'll provide you with strength
that Satan can't rattle
So sing out His praises
no matter the pain
and remember with Christ
you have only to gain
Like gold through the fire
completely refined
He'll bring you through shining
and with Him entwined*

The Gift of Singing

I sing in the car
I sing in the shower
When I sing to you
I feel your power
Your grace and your love
flow through me
As words pour forth
in a sweet melody
I don't see anyone
else but you
As your grace fills me
through and through
Thank you for
the gift of singing
With each note
your praises ringing
With each song
that fills the air
May all who hear them
find you there

Singing Praises

*Soft voices float
on the breeze
Blend in harmony
drifting through the trees
Mingle with music
and skip to the sky
Then fall on the Lord's ears
before they die
Precious little hymns
of praise
Singing all throughout
our days
Worshiping the Lord
on high
I'll praise him 'til
the day I die
Then in heaven
I will be
singing praises
for eternity*

ON
FAMILY AND FRIENDS

If one falls down, his friend can help him up. But pity the man who falls and has no one to help him up! Also if two lie down together they will keep warm. But how can one keep warm alone? Though one may be overpowered, two can defend themselves. A chord of three strands is not quickly broken.
Ecclesiastes 4:10-12

Life Lessons

Laughter and giggles
Singing a tune
Curling up on the couch
With Goodnight Moon
One Fish Two Fish
Sam I Am
Fox In Socks
And Green Eggs and Ham
Stopping to snuggle
and taking the time
to teach them these morals
In cute little rhymes
But don't forget
to take a look
At the most
important book
Read from the Bible
Teach them His ways
and help them prepare
for the rest of their days
Now you lay them down to sleep
Kiss them softly
and pray they'll keep
all these things within their heart
and take them with them
when you part

He Is My Son

*From sweet and charming
to anger and fears
Hugs and kisses
to kicking and tears
So many things
bottled inside
he can't explain
control, or hide
Autism is what they say
you have to take it
day by day
Cause each ones different
than the one before
You never know
what's in store
Lord please be with him
in all he may do
Hold him and guide him
and keep him with you
Every night my prayer will be
for loving patience
Cause you see
This child is not just anyone
This little boy
He is my son*

You Were Right

As we have our children
we often tend to see
The things that our parents said
somehow come to be
We swore that they were wrong
That we knew everything
They would see how right we were
Our praises they would sing
Oh they sing our praises
just not how we'd thought
It's when they see us with our kids
and we remember what they taught
We say things that sound like them
that we swore we'd never say
They laugh at us and shake their heads
as though they waited for this day
When we ourselves become parents
we see our parents in a different light
and yes I have to admit it
Mom and Dad you were right

Sending Off with Love

Little feet that patter
running to and fro
breathing deep and sighing
where does the time go
Chubby finger smudges
trailing down the halls
Bright crayon pictures
covering the walls
Oh Lord that we may teach them
All they need to know
To live life to it's fullest
And in Christ to grow
For all too soon they grow up
We marvel at the sight
Once again we're troubled
With many sleepless nights
As they venture on their own
We pray to God above
That they remember what they've learned
And send them off with love

God's Special People

God sends special people
to help along the way
When we get discouraged
they know just what to say
When they don't have the words
it's always good to know
That they will be there for you
To help you as you go
God calls special people
to help each other mend
He calls us His children
We call each other
FRIEND

God's Angels

When you least expect it
when you feel that no one cares
God sends out his angels
to remind us that He's there
They don't have golden halos
or wings as white as snow
They don't wear robes or play a harp
or fly wherever they go
They look just like you and I
the only difference being
They have a selfless heart of love
and a special way of seeing
They see the needs that others have
they reach out in Christ's love
They have a special tenderness
just like a graceful dove
God sends out his angels
just to let us know
That He is always with us
no matter where we go

It's Your Choice, My Friend

*You work all day
and night without ceasing
your worry and doubt
steadily increasing
You don't have time
to enjoy the day
You must make more
there's bills to pay
It's then that you realize
there's got to be more
Just what am I doing
all of this for?
Is happiness found
in having more stuff?
Would it make my life better
if I just made enough?
Whose definition
do we use to define?
enough can be different
in amount and kind
Do you have enough
to eat and to drink?
Do you have a bed,
a bathroom, a sink?
Do you have the love*

(continued)

*of family and friends?
Can you take it all with you
when life on Earth ends?
Is it better to have
a house full of things
or a heart full of love
and the peace that it brings?
Which leaves you richer
when it's all said and done?
Which of these things
brought you more fun?
Was it material things
that you worked hard to get?
Or the time spent with
loved one's without regret?
This choice my friend
is for you to make
You must choose
which path you will take
Will you place your focus
on getting more and more
or sit back and relax
and see what God has in store?*

In Your Own World

In your own world
Unable to cope
Not sure how to handle
the emotional slope
The ups and the downs
that change with a snap
The smiles and giggles
and off beat claps
People who stare
and roll their eyes
Not understanding
just how hard he tries
I would take his place
if only I could
But the Lord knows things
that only He should
He makes us different
to fulfill his plan
So I'll trust Him to care
as only He can